# NEW YORK, NEW YORK!

## The Big Apple from A to Z

By Laura Krauss Melmed • Illustrated by Frané Lessac

Collins

An Imprint of HarperCollinsPublishers

In memory of my mother, a New York girl
as vibrant as the city she loved
— L.K.M.

For Mom and Dad
— F.L.

Collins is an imprint of HarperCollins Publishers.

New York, New York! The Big Apple from A to Z
Text copyright © 2005 by Laura Krauss Melmed • Illustrations copyright © 2005 by Frané Lessac
Manufactured in China.

Library of Congress Cataloging-in-Publication Data
Melmed, Laura Krauss.
New York, New York! : the Big Apple from A to Z / by Laura Krauss Melmed ;
illustrated by Frané Lessac.— 1st ed.    p.  cm.    ISBN 978-0-06-054874-2 (trade bdg.)
ISBN 978-0-06-054876-6 (lib. bdg.) — ISBN 978-0-06-054877-3 (pbk.)
1. New York (N.Y.)—Juvenile literature. 2. English language—Alphabet—Juvenile literature. I. Lessac, Frané. II. Title.
F128.33.M45 2005   2004006495   974.7'1—dc22   CIP   AC

Typography by Stephanie Bart-Horvath
15 16 SCP 20 19 18 17 16 15
❖
First Edition

# WELCOME!

IMAGINE CLIMBING up to the top of a red double-decker bus in the heart of New York City. You are about to explore a city built by dreamers and workers, bankers and artists, Native Americans and immigrants from all over the world.

Manhattan Island was once the home of the Lenni Lenape Indians, whose ancestors had been settled there for 12,000 years. When Henry Hudson sailed across the Atlantic to explore the New World in 1609, he navigated the river that was later named after him, and the Lenape came out to greet him. Dutch settlers soon started a colony on Manhattan Island, calling it New Amsterdam. Because the Indians had no custom of owning, buying, or selling land, they eventually agreed to trade Manhattan Island to the Dutch for twenty-four dollars' worth of items such as knives and axes. Later the English took over the colony, changing its name to New York.

Today New York City is the largest, busiest, and most exciting metropolis in the United States. Each of its five boroughs—Manhattan, Queens, Brooklyn, the Bronx, and Staten Island—offers unique neighborhoods, fascinating museums, shady parks, and more!

Do you live in or near New York City? Then you can visit the places described here. If home is elsewhere, you can explore New York through these pages, or use the book to plan or remember an actual trip. In any case, get ready to open wide and take a juicy bite of the Big Apple—as we tour New York from A to Z!

# American Museum of Natural History

Whether you are interested in paleontology (the study of ancient living things), anthropology (the study of people and culture), or ichthyology (the study of fish), there will be something to interest you at the American Museum of Natural History.

View a giant *Barosaurus*
And colossal carved canoe.
Climb a tree to find small creatures,
As a scientist might do.
Navigate beneath the ocean;
Take a walk with early man.
Travel back in time and be there
When the universe began.

The museum has over 32 million specimens and objects relating to natural history.

In the 1860s, scientist Albert Bickmore came up with the idea to create the American Museum of Natural History. President Ulysses S. Grant took part in the 1874 groundbreaking for the new building on Central Park West.

The earliest known dinosaurs appeared about 228 million years ago. They dominated Earth for 163 million years. Modern humans have only been around for about 130,000 years!

Take a virtual tour through the Milky Way and all the way to the edge of the observable universe, using the digital dome system in the Space Theater.

The 50-foot-tall *Barosaurus* is rearing up to protect its baby from an attacking *Allosaurus*. This is the tallest freestanding dinosaur exhibit on Earth.

**TO THE SPACE THEATER**

# Brooklyn Bridge

No one ever had constructed
Such a massive bridge before
When John Roebling pledged he'd build one
From New York to Brooklyn's shore.
After thirteen years of labor
This great highway in the air
Spans the swift East River currents—
One man's vision brought to bear.

When John Roebling presented his design
for the Brooklyn Bridge to a group of
businessmen in 1867, it was the world's
longest suspension bridge. Begun in 1870,
it was finished in 1883.

Approximately 14,000 miles of wire
were used to wrap the suspension
cables. From end to end the bridge
spans 3,460 feet. The roadway is 135
feet above the water.

In 1870 Brooklyn was
the fastest-growing city
in the United States.

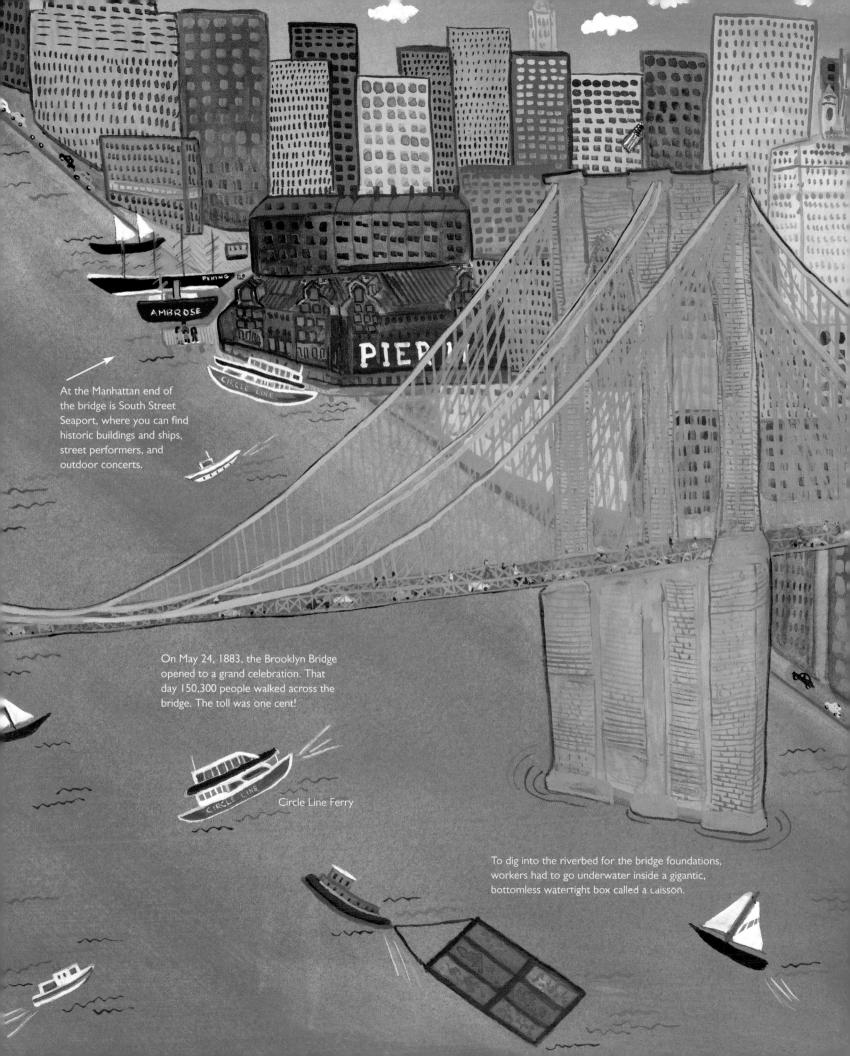

At the Manhattan end of the bridge is South Street Seaport, where you can find historic buildings and ships, street performers, and outdoor concerts.

PEKING

AMBROSE

PIER

CIRCLE LINE

On May 24, 1883, the Brooklyn Bridge opened to a grand celebration. That day 150,300 people walked across the bridge. The toll was one cent!

CIRCLE LINE

Circle Line Ferry

To dig into the riverbed for the bridge foundations, workers had to go underwater inside a gigantic, bottomless watertight box called a caisson.

# Central Park

You'll find hundreds of green acres
And a zillion things to do:
Skating, rowing, horseback riding,
And the carousel and zoo.

Central Park covers 6 percent of Manhattan. It has
26,000 trees, 21 playgrounds, and 8,968 benches.

Central Park North

Hudson River

Jacqueline Kennedy Onassis Reservoir

Great Lawn

Loeb Boathouse

Dairy

Zoo

Carousel

In the 1850s the Dairy brought in fresh milk from farms outside the city and sold it to children visiting Central Park.

# The Dairy

There are puppet shows and ball games,
Plays and concerts after dark,
And the Dairy, where kids once came
To drink milk in Central Park.

Guggenheim
Museum

This statue of Alice in Wonderland at the Mad Hatter's tea party is 11 feet tall.

There are 58 hand-carved, painted horses on the Carousel.

Metropolitan
Museum of
Art

Alice in
Wonderland
Statue

Boating
Pond

From March through October, visitors can rent rowboats from the Loeb Boathouse.

Central Park South

In the famous movie *King Kong*, a giant gorilla holds a woman captive on top of the Empire State Building.

The Empire State Building is struck by lightning about 100 times each year.

# Empire State Building

At this quarter-mile-high building

Find an 80-mile-wide view

All the way to Massachusetts

And to Pennsylvania, too.

Looking down, you'll see toy taxis

On the avenue below,

Rolling past the teeny people,

Who, like ants, rush to and fro.

Skywalkers, Iroquois Indians skilled at working at great heights, built the steel frame of the Empire State Building and of almost every other large building and bridge in New York.

It is said that the architects got the idea for the Empire State Building from looking at a pencil.

The Empire State Building's annual lighting schedule honors seasons, holidays, and events. The top of the building shines yellow on Easter and blue and orange on the opening day of the Knicks. It shines white between holidays.

About 35,000 people a day go to the Empire State Building to work, do errands, or enjoy the observation deck on the building's 86th floor.

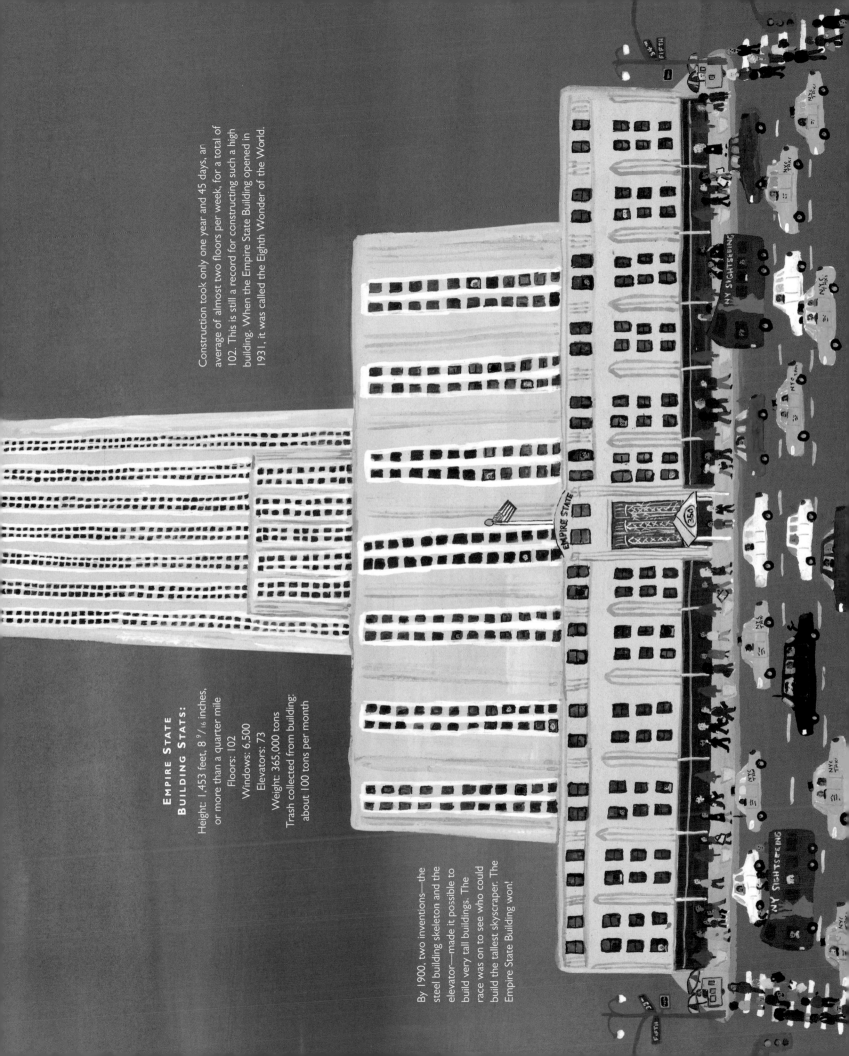

## EMPIRE STATE BUILDING STATS:

Height: 1,453 feet, 8 9/16 inches,
or more than a quarter mile

Floors: 102
Windows: 6,500
Elevators: 73
Weight: 365,000 tons
Trash collected from building:
about 100 tons per month

Construction took only one year and 45 days, an average of almost two floors per week, for a total of 102. This is still a record for constructing such a high building. When the Empire State Building opened in 1931, it was called the Eighth Wonder of the World.

By 1900, two inventions—the steel building skeleton and the elevator—made it possible to build very tall buildings. The race was on to see who could build the tallest skyscraper. The Empire State Building won!

# Fifth Avenue

On Fifth Avenue go shopping,
Ride a horse-drawn cab, or hop
On a double-decker bus tour.
(Don't forget to sit up top!)
Wear a kooky hat on Easter,
Be it store-bought or homemade,
And join all the folks out strolling
In the Easter Day parade.

Fifth Avenue hosts parades on holidays such as St. Patrick's Day, Columbus Day, and Easter. During the Easter Parade, people in fancy clothing, costumes, and amazing hats gather around St. Patrick's Cathedral.

Fifth Avenue starts at Washington Square in Greenwich Village and stretches all the way to Harlem.

Built in 1902, the Flatiron Building is the oldest remaining skyscraper in New York.

The New York Public Library on Fifth Avenue is one of more than 200 public libraries in New York City.

The Museum of Modern Art showcases over 100,000 pieces of art.

On Diamond Row (47th Street off Fifth Avenue), nearly every shop glitters with diamonds and gold jewelry.

Rockefeller Center is made up of 19 buildings.

During the winter holidays, crowds line up to view the famous window displays at Saks.

St. Patrick's Cathedral is the largest gothic-style Catholic cathedral in the United States.

Each piece of jewelry from Tiffany's is packaged in a signature blue box.

The luxurious Plaza Hotel is located at the southeast corner of Central Park.

# Grand Central Terminal

New York's fabulous Grand Central
Is the queen of railway stations.
Her main concourse most majestic
Wears a crown of constellations.
There's a special place to whisper,
Sweeping staircase, marble floor,
And the Roman god of travel,
Who keeps watch above the door.

The great arched windows on the east and west walls have walkways.

The double staircase is modeled on one in another landmark structure, the Paris Opera building.

Grand Central was built in the early 1900s as a gateway to New York, in a time when trains were the fastest and most popular way to travel.

The whispering gallery

SHUTTLE 42 STREET    PARCEL ROOM

TICKETS

HARLEM  HUDSON  NEWHAVEN  TICKETS

NEW HAVEN DEPARTURES  ALL TRAIN ARRIVALS    HARLEM HUDSON DEPARTURES

TIME TRACK

5:00    37
5:04    21
5:08    108
5:14    115
5:24    26
5:27
5:29    20
5:31    30
5:39    41
5:47    37
5:47    21

The ceiling shows the constellations of the zodiac, copied from a medieval manuscript.

A 50-foot statue of the Roman god Mercury stands atop the clock at the main entrance. Mercury was the speedy messenger of the gods and is also the fastest-moving and innermost planet of our solar system.

The main concourse is about 275 feet long by about 120 feet wide and 125 feet high.

Over half a million people come and go through Grand Central Terminal each day.

TO VANDERBILT AVENUE AND TAXIS

THE CAFE AT GRAND CENTRAL

LOWER LEVEL TRACKS 100-117

OYSTER BAR

INFORMATION

TRACK 29

TRACK 28

The Manhattan Indians called Harlem "Muscoota," or flat place. Later, Dutch farmers named it "Nieuw Haarlem" after a city in the Netherlands. The English later changed the name to Harlem.

## Harlem

From the famed Apollo Theater
To the house of Langston Hughes,
From the sounds of jazz and gospel
To the hip-hop beat and blues,
From Caribbean to soul food
To West African cuisine,
There's a neighborhood called Harlem
To be tasted, heard, and seen.

During the Harlem Renaissance in the 1920s, writers such as Langston Hughes flocked to Harlem along with African American painters, actors, dancers, and musicians to explore and celebrate black roots and culture.

Harlem is located in uptown Manhattan. In 1832 the New York and Harlem Railroad Company linked lower Manhattan to Harlem, allowing many immigrants to move there from downtown. African Americans began moving there in such great numbers that it became the largest African American community in the United States.

Music has always been a major part of Harlem's cultural life. In 1934 the Apollo Theater introduced Amateur Night and launched the careers of many legendary artists. Today the Apollo continues to host many famous musicians.

APOLLO

IT'S STILL LIVE AT THE APOLLO

APPEARING TONIGHT
JAMES BROWN  LAURYN HILL
BILLIE HOLIDAY  THE SUPREMES
ELLA FITZGERALD  PRINCE
DUKE ELLINGTON  BILL COSBY

The Tree of Hope once stood by the Lafayette Theater. Performers touched it for good luck before going onstage. When the street was widened, the tree had to be cut down. But a piece of its wood was preserved backstage at the Apollo.

# Intrepid

The Concorde is the world's only supersonic passenger aircraft. It can cruise at more than twice the speed of sound and maintain an altitude of up to 60,000 feet. The Concorde was in service for twenty-seven years, and one is now displayed on a barge next to the *Intrepid*.

Harrier

Tracer

Falcon

Tomcat

Tiger

The *Intrepid*'s flight simulators reproduce the thrill of flying an F/A 18 Hornet at mach speed or guiding a supersonic jet plane between mountain peaks.

This huge vessel called *Intrepid*
Has some rousing tales to tell—
Sailing steadfast into battle,
She fulfilled her mission well.
She has carried planes and 'copters
Through two wars, courageously—
Now she proudly stands to honor
All who bravely serve at sea.

The U.S.S. *Intrepid* served the U.S. Navy for 31 years. In World War II she suffered seven bombing attacks, five kamikaze strikes, and one torpedo hit. Because she kept returning to action after being repaired, enemies nicknamed her the "Ghost Ship."

In the 1960s NASA used the *Intrepid* as a recovery vessel for spaceships. Replicas of these space capsules can be found at an exhibit called Mission Control.

Hudson River

CIRCLE LINE

U.S.S. *Edison*

946

The U.S.S. *Growler* is the only complete strategic nuclear missile submarine in the world that is open to the public. Tours give visitors a firsthand look at life aboard a submarine and a close-up view of the once top secret missile command center.

Skywarrior

577

NAVY

Vigilante

Demon

U.S.S. *Growler*

NAVY

Intruder II

Blackbird

NAVY

Corsair II

Cobra

The *Intrepid* is 900 feet long. Visitors to the Intrepid Sea-Air-Space Museum can tour the flight and hangar decks, the aircraft, the Combat Information Center with its radar scopes, the island and bridges, the captain's sea quarters, and many exhibits on flight, the navy, space, and military technology.

# Jones Beach

When the summer sidewalks sizzle,
There's a cool place close at hand
To go swimming in the ocean
Or build castles in the sand.
Reached by car or bus or railroad,
It's the perfect destination
For a not-far-from-the-city,
One-day, sun-and-surf vacation.

Jones Beach is a state park on Long Island, about 33 miles from New York City. It covers over 2,400 acres, including eight ocean beaches stretching over 6 miles.

The park is named for Major Thomas Jones, who ran a whaling station in this area around 1700.

JONES BEACH

Jones Beach opened to the public in 1929. Huge crowds come to swim, fish, or go boating, to play softball, basketball, or miniature golf, or to roller-skate. There are bird-watching areas, a boardwalk, and concerts held at night in the Jones Beach Amphitheater.

To John F. Kennedy International Airport

In July, the hottest month of the year, the average temperature at Jones Beach is 74 degrees.

To create Jones Beach, the parks commission trucked in tons of sand, created dunes, and planted beach grass to hold them in place.

The Knicks' team colors are the official colors of New York City: orange, blue, and white.

## Knicks

In New York there is a garden
Where no tree or flower grows,
A spectacular arena
That hosts sports events and shows.
Here the Knicks play all their home games
(Tickets sell out 1-2-3!)
And the fans go wild each summer
For a team called Liberty.

Madison Square Garden seats 20,000 fans.

When a great player retires, his number is sometimes retired too, and his jersey is hung from the rafters alongside banners for NBA titles. The first Knicks player who got this honor was Walt Frazier, number 10. Other retired numbers include number 24, Bill Bradley (later elected to the United States Senate), and number 33, Patrick Ewing.

The New York Knickerbockers, or "Knicks" for short, were named after Father Knickerbocker, a popular symbol of New York City. He wore a three-cornered hat, buckled shoes, and short rolled-up pants that the Dutch settlers called "knickerbockers."

Daily tours of Madison Square Garden go behind the scenes and to the team locker rooms. Visitors can see what goes into preparing for a live game or show, and learn things like how a basketball court turns into an ice rink.

The Garden has hosted tennis tournaments, boxing bouts, dog shows, concerts, ice shows, and circuses.

# Lincoln Center

Think Lincoln Center's just for grown-ups?
Not a chance, for on its stages
You'll find music, dance, and movies
Geared to children of all ages:

The immense horseshoe-shaped auditorium of the Metropolitan Opera House has red-velvet walls and seats where visitors can watch operas performed on one of five moveable stages.

New York State Theater

Metropolitan Opera House

Each fall and winter the Big Apple Circus pitches its tent next to the Metropolitan Opera House, in Damrosch Park.

The New York City Ballet trains its own dancers and creates its own ballets. It even has its own costume shop, where 18 people work, including a tutu expert.

Lincoln Center is bigger than 12 football fields put together.

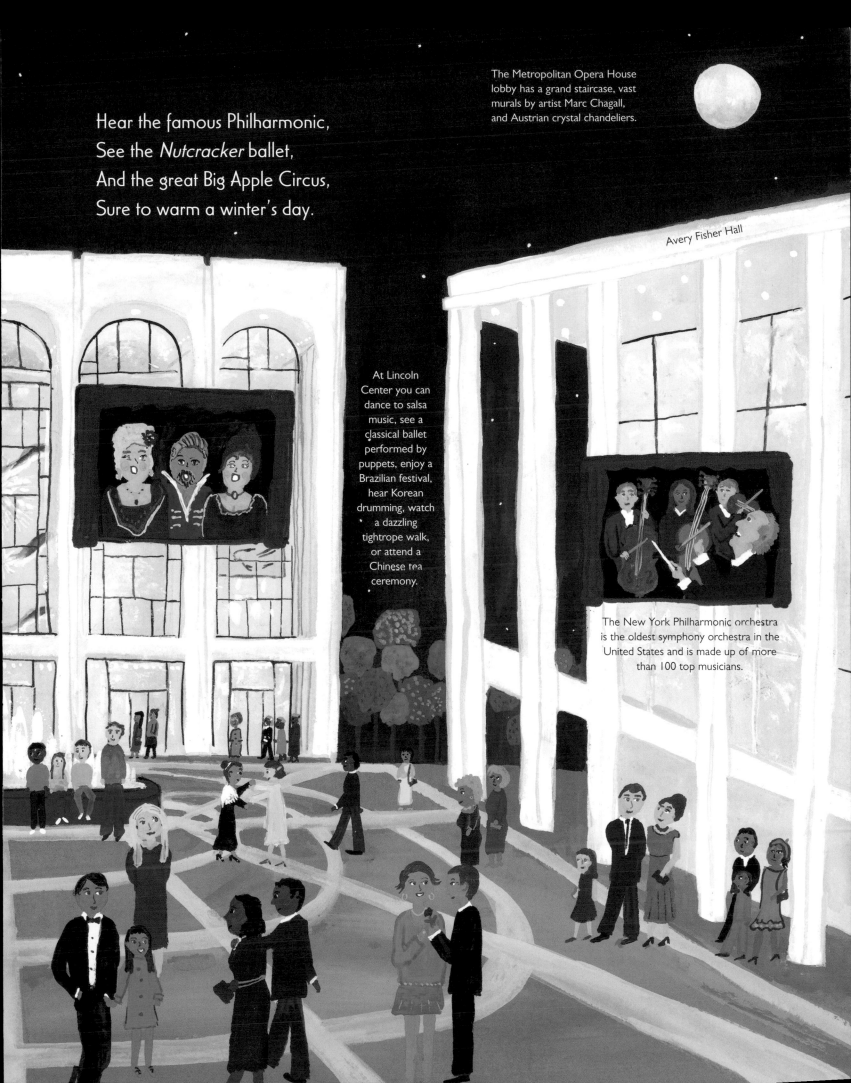

Hear the famous Philharmonic,
See the *Nutcracker* ballet,
And the great Big Apple Circus,
Sure to warm a winter's day.

The Metropolitan Opera House lobby has a grand staircase, vast murals by artist Marc Chagall, and Austrian crystal chandeliers.

Avery Fisher Hall

At Lincoln Center you can dance to salsa music, see a classical ballet performed by puppets, enjoy a Brazilian festival, hear Korean drumming, watch a dazzling tightrope walk, or attend a Chinese tea ceremony.

The New York Philharmonic orchestra is the oldest symphony orchestra in the United States and is made up of more than 100 top musicians.

# Metropolitan Museum of Art

See a whole Egyptian temple,
Mummies big and mummies small,
Rooms chock-full of arms and armor,
And a painting twelve feet tall,
Baseball cards, a sculpture garden,
Films for kids, and don't forget
To find William the Blue Hippo,
Little mascot of the Met.

The first object acquired by the museum was a Roman sarcophagus, or coffin.

Classical Greek statues

A pendant mask from Benin made in the 1700s

*Cypresses* is by Vincent van Gogh, a now famous artist who was only able to sell one painting in his lifetime!

William the Hippo is only 8 inches long.

The Metropolitan Museum of Art was started in 1870 to provide ordinary people with a place to view and learn about great works of art.

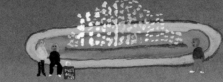

The museum has more than 3 million objects in its collections. If you took a minute to look at each object without taking a break, it would take you almost five years to see them all!

← Downtown

The Arms and Armor collection has more than 15,000 objects from many countries covering 23 centuries.

The Egyptian Temple of Dendur was built around 15 B.C.E. to honor the goddess Isis.

This painted coffin of Henettawy, an ancient Egyptian woman, shows her dressed in a wig and jewelry designed to be worn after her death.

Measuring more than 12 feet by 21 feet, *Washington Crossing the Delaware* by Emanuel Leutze is the largest framed painting on canvas at the Met.

The back of the Met faces Central Park.

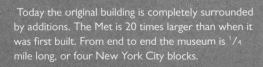

Today the original building is completely surrounded by additions. The Met is 20 times larger than when it was first built. From end to end the museum is ¹/₄ mile long, or four New York City blocks.

Fifth Avenue

Uptown ⟶

# New York Fire Museum

New York's finest, New York's bravest:
They are heroes of our streets
Whether making daring rescues
Or patrolling daily beats.

All New York firefighters were volunteers until 1865, when the paid Metropolitan Fire Department was started.

In 1731 New York got its first two fire trucks from England. Before that, fires were fought by bucket brigade, a line of people passing pails of water hand to hand.

Firefighters at the World Trade Center site, September 11, 2001

# New York Police Museum

Fighting crime or fighting fires,
They are two courageous teams!
Find out all the facts about them
When you visit their museums.

The first NYPD badge was shaped like a star. It was made of copper, which explains why people started calling police "cops." Today's badge is shaped like a shield and is made from copper, nickel, and zinc.

Police at the World Trade Center site, September 11, 2001

Uniformed police dress in blue, and police detectives dress in "plain clothes."

Undercover police dress and act so they can blend in with a group of people.

NEW YORK CITY POLICE MUSEUM

POLICE STATION

FIRST PRECINCT

NYPD ▾ POLICE

POLICE

The NYPD Mounted Unit has six divisions of troops who patrol streets and parks on horseback.

The Lower East Side's Tenement Museum takes visitors back through time into the restored apartments of 97 Orchard Street.

In the 1800s the Lower East Side became the most crowded neighborhood in the world.

# Orchard Street

To these crowded streets named Orchard,
Ludlow, Hester, Broome, and Grand
Immigrants have flocked for decades
From their homes in distant lands.
They have journeyed here to settle,
Seeking opportunity
And the chance to raise their children
In a country that is free.

A tenement is a house that can hold more than one family.

Orchard Street once ran through the orchards of wealthy landowner James DeLancey.

GURVITZ
CLOTHING

SIEGELS
KOSHER BUTCHER

שש

A large Jewish community
thrived on the Lower East Side
for more than 100 years.

UNION HATS

Orchard Street was known for its
many pushcarts—outdoor wagons that
sold low-priced clothing and food to
swarms of eager shoppers.

LOUIS
MOISHE

A. KAMEL TIPS
Shoelaces

Pickles
5¢

# Plaza Hotel

*Dahhhling*, meet me at the Plaza,
At a quarter after three.
We'll wear pearls and order ice cream,
Plates of fancy cakes, and tea.

In 1969 the Plaza was listed on the Register of Historic Places. It is the only New York City hotel to be designated as a National Historic Landmark.

58th Street

59th Street

Fifth Avenue

I'll be waiting in the lobby
Underneath a chandelier,
So come meet me at the Plaza,
On Fifth Avenue, my dear!

The Plaza Hotel first opened in 1907. The 19-story, 805-room building looks out over Central Park and Fifth Avenue and is one of the most elegant hotels in the world.

The Deluxe Aristocratic Afternoon Tea menu at the Plaza's Palm Court restaurant includes caviar, smoked salmon, sandwiches, desserts, and an assortment of teas.

The largest single order in history for gold-encrusted china dinnerware was placed with Straus & Sons for the Plaza restaurants. The Plaza also bought 1,650 crystal chandeliers.

At first the Plaza was home to well-to-do New Yorkers such as the Vanderbilts. Later the apartments were turned into luxury hotel suites. Many famous guests came to stay at the Plaza, including author Mark Twain, architect Frank Lloyd Wright, and the Beatles.

At the end of the 1920s, John D. Rockefeller set out to build 14 buildings around a central plaza. Rockefeller Center covers 11 acres and stretches from 49th to 52nd Street and from Fifth to Seventh Avenue.

# Q Train

There are 22 stops on the Q train, which runs from Brighton Beach in Brooklyn to 57th Street and Seventh Avenue in Manhattan.

Take the Q train to Manhattan
Where, on clear December nights,
Magic shimmers in shop windows
And the streets are dressed in lights.

The giant Christmas tree is usually a Norway spruce at least 65 feet tall and 35 feet wide.

The tree is hung with 25,000 bulbs strung over 5 miles of wire.

This statue depicts Atlas, who carries the heavens upon his shoulders as punishment for defying Zeus.

In 1936 the skating rink, then a daring experiment, was made possible because of a new invention: refrigeration.

# Rockefeller Center

Stroll through Rockefeller Center,
Watch the skaters gliding by,
See the Christmas tree and Atlas,
Whose broad back supports the sky.

The New York City subway system has 656 miles of track, 468 stations, and 31,180 turnstiles. The first line opened in 1904.

# Statue of Liberty

As a sign of hope and freedom
She is held in great renown:
She's the lady of the harbor
With her torch and shining crown.
Ellis Island is her neighbor,
Where, till 1954,
Immigrants to New York City
First set foot upon this shore.

The seven rays of the statue's crown stand for the seven continents and seven seas.

The Statue of Liberty was a gift to the United States from France to celebrate the 100th anniversary of the Declaration of Independence.

French sculptor Frederic Auguste Bartholdi modeled the face of the Statue of Liberty after his mother's. The internal structure was designed by Alexandre Gustave Eiffel, designer of the Eiffel Tower in Paris.

← To New Jersey

**STATUE STATS:**

Height: 151 feet, 1 inch
Index finger: 8 feet long
Nose: 4 feet 6 inches
from top to tip
Steps to the crown: 354

In her left hand Lady Liberty holds a tablet. It says in Roman numerals, "JULY IV MDCCLXXVI" — July 4, 1776—the date of America's independence from Great Britain.

the Staten Island Ferry
CITY OF NEW YORK

CIRCLE LINE

Bedloe's Island, the site of an old fort in New York Harbor, was chosen as the place where the statue would stand. It was renamed Liberty Island in 1956.

To Manhattan

From 1892 to 1954 over 12 million immigrants entered the United States through Ellis Island, neighbor to Liberty Island in New York Harbor. Most came from Europe in one of the greatest mass movements of people in history.

the Staten Island Ferry  CITY OF NEW YORK

At the Ellis Island Immigration Museum visitors can experience the place where their ancestors first stepped onto United States soil. The American Immigrant Wall of Honor shows the names of more than 500,000 immigrant Americans.

CIRCLE LINE

The completed statue was broken down into 350 pieces, packed in crates, and sent to the United States by ship. It was placed on its pedestal inside the star-shaped walls of the old Fort Wood. With fireworks, speeches, and boats filling the harbor, thousands of people watched as the Statue of Liberty was dedicated on October 28, 1886.

To Brooklyn

Times Square is located where Broadway cuts across Seventh Avenue at 42nd Street.

The first New Year's Eve ball–dropping ceremony took place in 1907. Today as many as 500,000 people squeeze into Times Square to ring in the New Year, and many millions more watch the ball drop on television.

Broadway is nicknamed the "Great White Way" because of all the neon lights.

An Indian path called the Wickquasgeck Road once ran the length of Manhattan Island. Later it became a street named Broadway because it was so wide.

# Times Square

House lights dim, the crowd grows quiet,
Notes are played, the footlights glow.
Now the velvet curtain rises—
You are at a Broadway show!
Just outside, the streets are hoppin',
Giant billboards blazing bright,
People, movies, taxis, restaurants—
Times Square never sleeps at night!

# U Union Square Greenmarket

Union Square was named this because it *unites* Broadway and Fourth Avenue.

HONEY    HONEY    PET GRASS    CATS

APPLES    APPLES    APPLES    PUMPKINS

On the south side of Manhattan
You will find two famous squares:
Union Square offers a market
Where the farmers sell fresh wares.

At greenmarkets around New York
City, shoppers can choose from among
47 different types of peas and beans,
120 types of apples, 120 types of
tomatoes, and 350 types of peppers.

During the 1820s streets in other parts of Manhattan were being laid out in straight lines. But the people of Greenwich Village got permission to keep their jumbled, crooked lanes. Since Village streets were too narrow for large buildings, they were, and still are, lined with smaller houses with tiny gardens and secret courtyards.

Washington Square Arch

Greenwich Village is the home of New York University.

Greenwich Village, often known as "the Village," was once a marshland. In the 1780s the city drained the swamp where Washington Square Park now stands.

## Village

Under Washington Square's archway
You may meet a mime or two
Plus magicians and musicians
Who'll perform their acts for you.

Many famous authors have lived in the Village, including Edgar Allan Poe and Mark Twain. The Village is a well-known gathering place for writers, artists, actors, and musicians.

# Wall Street

Hop a taxi down to Wall Street,
Where the stock exchange is found
And where bulls and bears are talked of
(Though none seem to be around).

When someone uses the term "bull market," it means prices of securities are rising. In a "bear market," prices of securities are going down.

The trading floor is 50 feet high and filled with the bustle and noise of traders. The Big Board is a huge electronic display that keeps track of the buying and selling.

This chart shows how one company's securities have changed over a year-long period.

| 52-Week High | Low | Stock | Div | Yld % | P/E |
|---|---|---|---|---|---|
| 63.88 | 35.31 | WX Comm | 1.76 | 3.9 | 15 |

Each taxi has a light on the roof. When it is lit, the taxi is available to pick up passengers. To a hail a cab, a person stands at the curb and sticks out an arm.

**TaXi**

Wall Street really *was* a walled street
In New Amsterdam of old—
Now, here, daily by the billions
Securities are bought and sold.

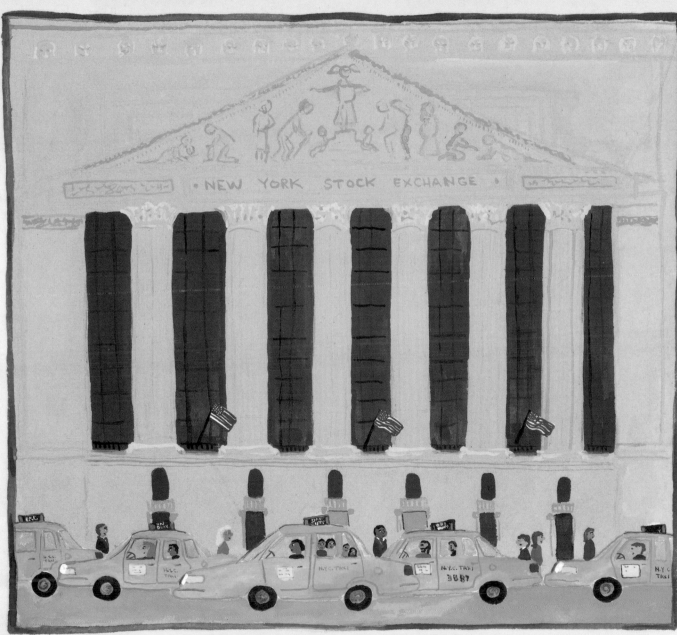

At the New York Stock Exchange, people buy and sell securities. Owning a security means you own a small part—a "share"—of a company such as Nike or Coca-Cola.

There are 12,187 yellow taxis in Manhattan. Adults who live there hail a cab an average of 100 times per year.

Wall Street is named after an actual wall that was built by the Dutch in 1653 to keep the British and Indians from attacking.

| Sales 100s | High | Low | Last | Chg |
|---|---|---|---|---|
| 15584 | 45.73 | 44.58 | 42.20 | -0.07 |

The Yankees hold the record for the most World Series Championships: 26 so far.

# Yankee Stadium

It is called "The House That Ruth Built,"
First constructed, people say,
So Babe Ruth, that Yankee legend,
Would have someplace grand to play.
At a Yankees game you'll mingle
With New Yorkers big and small
As they yell and cheer while watching
The Bronx Bombers playing ball.

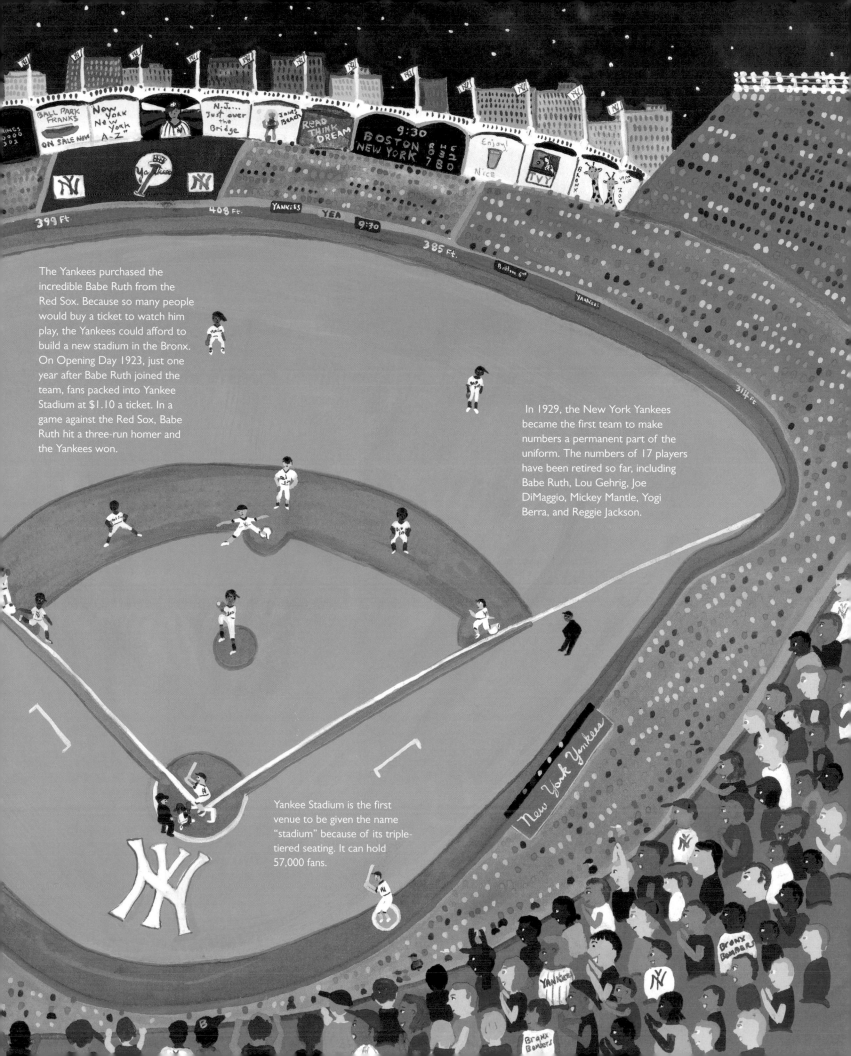

The Yankees purchased the incredible Babe Ruth from the Red Sox. Because so many people would buy a ticket to watch him play, the Yankees could afford to build a new stadium in the Bronx. On Opening Day 1923, just one year after Babe Ruth joined the team, fans packed into Yankee Stadium at $1.10 a ticket. In a game against the Red Sox, Babe Ruth hit a three-run homer and the Yankees won.

In 1929, the New York Yankees became the first team to make numbers a permanent part of the uniform. The numbers of 17 players have been retired so far, including Babe Ruth, Lou Gehrig, Joe DiMaggio, Mickey Mantle, Yogi Berra, and Reggie Jackson.

Yankee Stadium is the first venue to be given the name "stadium" because of its triple-tiered seating. It can hold 57,000 fans.

# Z Bronx Zoo

The Bronx Zoo covers hundreds of acres and is home to more than 4,000 animals.

Many animals are in large outdoor areas set up like their natural habitats. These areas include the African Plains, Congo Gorilla Forest, and Tiger Mountain.

Each zebra stripe pattern is as individual as a human fingerprint.

For over 100 years, The Wildlife Conservation Society has worked from its headquarters at the Bronx Zoo to understand and protect wild animals and their habitats. The WCS has saved countless species and created parks and reserves all around the world.

The Skyfari cable cars soar over the park. There is also a tram and a Bengali Express monorail in Wild Asia.

A safari in the city?
Sounds fantastic but it's true—
Many animals roam freely
In this different sort of zoo.
Visit jungles, World of Darkness,
The Baboon Reserve, and more!
Start with apes and end with zebras
On your Bronx safari tour.

Giraffe babies may be up to 6 feet tall at birth.

Zoo goers can watch the animal keepers exercise with sea lions, feed the tigers, and toss live crickets to birds called carmine bee-eaters.

A American Museum of Natural History

B Brooklyn Bridge

C Central Park

D Dairy

E Empire State Building

F Fifth Avenue

G Grand Central Terminal

H Harlem

I Intrepid

J Jones Beach

K Knicks

L Lincoln Center

M Metropolitan Museum of Art

N New York Fire Museum/Police Museum

O Orchard Street

P Plaza Hotel

Q Q Train

R Rockefeller Center

S Statue of Liberty

T Times Square

U Union Square Greenmarket

V Village

W Wall Street

X TaXi

Y Yankee Stadium

Z Bronx Zoo

THE BRONX

MANHATTAN

NEW JERSEY

Hudson River

East River

QUEENS

BROOKLYN

Ellis Island

STATEN ISLAND

To Atlantic Ocean

To Jones Beach